Survivor

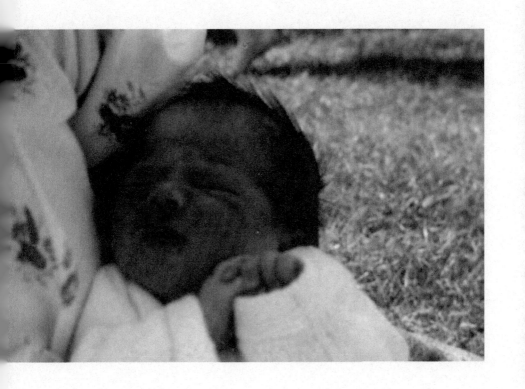

Me and Murph

"Hey you there ooh"

Prologue

This is what I was told.

On the 11th April 1996 is was foggy. It was half term at the time and I was at the stables with my friends.

When it was time to get the ponies in, a lady from the stables came with me. We weren't wearing our riding hats.

We opened the gate and I went to get my pony in. You're supposed to walk to your pony but the lady from the stables called hers instead.

All the horse and ponies in the paddock started galloping to the gate as it was so cold and they wanted to come in.

I don't know if the lady from the stables managed to get her pony out of the paddock but I was still in there.

As it was foggy, the ponies and horses couldn't see me and I couldn't see them. Suddenly a horse came galloping past me, kicked out and caught my head. I was knocked unconscious.

If we'd have been wearing riding hats and the lady from stables hadn't called her pony in, my life wouldn't have changed.

Contents

Chapter 1

Growing up - my early memories (1982-1995)

By Katie

This is a true story.

I will be telling you all about my life and how it was shattered by a serious brain injury. You'll also be hearing about the impact it had on my family. Their lives changed forever that day as well.

I'll start by describing my life before the day it changed forever.

I was born in Boston, a town in Lincolnshire, on the 25th June 1982, very early in the morning.

I lived in a farm house in a village called Sutterton with my Mum, Dad and my older Sister.

I had a great, happy life. We had horse called Barney, a Labrador called Murphy, a cat (I can't remember the name) and some chickens.

The house was big with a huge garden. We had stables, a barn and two paddocks to ride in.

As I was growing up, I used to love riding Barney, but it wasn't always easy!

I remember riding him in the paddock once. Something spooked Barney and he bolted, galloping as fast as he could in a blind panic. I ended up hitting my head on a tree and falling off. Thankfully, I had my riding helmet on so I wasn't seriously hurt.

My best friend growing up was a girl called Hannah. She lived really near to our farm and we were both born on the same day.

We would both play at each other's houses and stay over all the time. I remember playing with Hannah in the paddock. The grass was so long it was like a maze! We also used to ride our bikes up the little roads to another farm we knew. We were the best of friends and went to the same primary school, where Hannah's Mum worked.

In around 1993 (when I was 11) we moved from the farm into Spalding. I had to move to another primary school which made me really sad.

Our horses from the farm were moved to a Livery Yard/Riding School. My Mum told me (although I don't remember) Barney had an epileptic fit and had to be put down while our other horse was eventually sold.

It was at this time that I got my own pony called Ensign.

I loved Ensign and we had great fun together! Dressage was my favourite and I remember being really happy one day after winning a competition.

I also tried cross-country although it wasn't really for me. I did a lot of training, going round to each jump on my lessons but on the day of the competition Ensign stopped at the first jump and I fell off!

I started at secondary school in 1994 and, like all kids, it was a big deal for me.

At first, everything was fine, but soon the bullying started. Other girls in the class used to gang up on me and say horrible things. The bullying made my life a misery and continued until I was in year 9.

I was on way home really upset one day and I told Mum that I didn't want to go back to school. My Mum and Dad went to see the head teacher but the school wouldn't do anything about it so I refused to go back to school.

I looked at three school different schools and eventually picked the one Claire, my Sister, went to. I loved my new school. I had lots of friends (one of the girls also liked horses), and my own pony. Then my life went horribly wrong.

Chapter 2

Katie's life changing injuries (1996)

Report by the Emergency Services

This is the first part of the report from Doctor Wiscombe who was a volunteer at 'LIVES' which stands for 'LINCOLNSHIRE INTEGRATED VOLUNTEER EMERGENCY SERVICES'.

On the 11th April 1996 whilst in the Accident & Emergency Department at the local Hospital, I received a call from Lincolnshire Ambulance Control requesting my attendance at a local equestrian centre, where it was reported that a young female had sustained a serious head injury following a riding accident.

It was a cold, foggy day, as I made haste to the incident location. I had the fortune of a dedicated rapid response medical vehicle fully equipped with audio and visual warnings.

I arrived on the scene just in advance of the emergency Ambulance. A 13-year-old girl, who I recognised as Katie, one of my patients in general practice, had been kicked in the head by a horse. She lay in the field, comforted by bystanders and covered in blankets. She was unconscious, although still breathing. There was massive open head injury to the left side of the head, with the left external ear being severely lacerated. In conjunction with the Ambulance crew, we stabilised Katie's condition, attending to her airway, breathing and circulation.

The Lincolnshire Air Ambulance had been requested to the scene and soon joined us. It was not long, therefore, before we had Katie evacuated from the scene and transferred to the local hospital.

Katie was seen in Casualty at her local hospital by the surgeons and was transferred from there to the Queen's Medical Centre in Nottingham, again by Air Ambulance. She was taken to the operating theatre that same day and a depressed fracture of one of the skull bones was elevated. She was found to have bruising on the brain and a large clot was evacuated. At the same time, her severely lacerated ear was repaired.

After the operation she was transferred to the Paediatric Intensive Care Unit, where ventilation continued for two weeks.

Initial attempts to remove Katie from life support failed because of the collapse of her right lower lung. However, eventually she came off ventilation and was transferred to the ward for rehabilitation. Although conscious, she remained detached, with no verbal response. Speech therapy and passive exercise of all her limbs were commenced and gradually limb movements returned. Although initially fed via a nasogastric tube, after three weeks Katie was able to tolerate free fluids. Katie continued to make good progress thereafter, despite some weakening of the right arm. She did, however, suffer from a form of complex aphasia (a brain disorder where a person has trouble speaking or understanding other people speaking). Great importance was attached to continuing physiotherapy, occupational therapy and speech therapy.

Katie suffered a generalised fit in September 1996 (5 months after the initial accident) because of her past head injury. As a consequence, she was started on anti-epileptic medication. I observed with great pleasure Katie's slow but progressive improvement. This was due to the efforts of all of those who attended to Katie, but particularly due to the determination of the family. Slowly but surely her speech and understanding of language returned and she made a complete recovery of her ability to use her limbs - a great tribute to all those involved in her care.

Chapter 3

Fighting for my life (1996)

By Katie

This is what I was told had happened the day after my accident.

Mr Punt, the neurosurgeon at Queen's Medical Centre and his assistant Maria had performed an operation to repair the fracture in my skull.

My left ear was also damaged and had to be stitched back on by a plastic surgeon.

I went to theatre at around 8pm and arrived back to the Intensive Care ward at 3pm the next day (12 April 1996). I had two tubes in my nose, one for eating and the other to help me breathe. There were lots of other wires attached to a computer which told the nurse about my heart, pulse and the pressure in my head.

A very close watch was kept on me overnight by my special nurse, Vicki.

The first 72 hours were critical and a very close watch was kept on the pressure in my head which showed on a monitor. If it rose above 30 there would be grave cause for concern. At one point, it rose to 32 - and then came down - everyone breathed a sigh of relief - but I wasn't out of the woods by a long way.

I spent the next two weeks in intensive care on a ventilator and in a coma.

I was monitored every half an hour by my special nurse Vicki to make sure that my condition was not getting worse.

I was having physio twice a day to make sure that my lungs didn't fill with fluid.

They tapped my chest first to loosen fluid, then inserted a tube down through my nose into the lung to try and draw off fluid. Despite this, on the 18th April 1996 my right lung collapsed and they had to drain off more fluid to get me going again. It was slow progress and just a waiting game. Eventually the X-ray of my lungs showed the fluid level was going down but they were all very worried about pneumonia setting in.

Mum and Dad sat at my bedside playing tapes and talking to me. Mum also washed me and read to me.

Over the next few days there was some improvement in my condition and the decision was made to take the ventilator away. This was hurriedly re-connected after it was plain that I could not manage.

My Sister came to see me with her boyfriend and Mum and Dad went home to collect more clothes. They came back the next day with my favourite duvet and best teddy.

Another attempt was made at taking me off the ventilator and this time it worked. At last, I could breathe on my own.

Maria arrived to take the bolt out of my head which was monitoring the pressure - another small step in the right direction. Gradually the Diazepam drug which was keeping me immobilised was reduced. Everyone waited with baited breath. The doctors told Mum and Dad that it should wear off within 24 hours but 30 hours later I still hadn't moved.

Encouragingly however, over the next few days various slight movements were noted and my eyes started to flicker open.

I was then introduced to liquid food through a tube. As I was now off the ventilator, on 25 April 1996 I was to be moved (this is still hard to say) to a high dependency neurological ward. Mum and Dad were both worried about this but doctors said that it was up to me now.

The feeding process through the tube had to be replaced every four hours and monitored all the time. One day the nurses said it was time to wash what was left on my hair, which was full of blood and dirt. They decided to put me in a hoist and take me to the bath. Apparently, I didn't like this but I couldn't do or say anything about it.

Mum and Dad continued to stay with me and did a lot of the day-to-day care. By this time, I had my eyes open and could move one leg very slightly. The physios still came round every day and mum was doing my exercises for me twice every day.

Mum had to bend my legs up and down six times, then my arms, and then push my feet up to flex my ankle. As the catheter had now been removed, I had to have nappies on and mum changed me when needed.

After I had settled down for a few days, the physios, Paula and Sarah, came to see me. They got me up to sit on the side of the bed whilst they propped me up. I didn't like this because my head was dizzy but I couldn't tell anyone.

The next step was getting me out into a chair. It was like an armchair with a special head prop and I could be wheeled about.

There were some hamsters in the ward and Mum wheeled me over to see them. She put them in my lap and put my hand on them. I was still not moving and so I had to be propped up in the chair and I showed no interest in anything.

The following week, three friends from the stables where I had the accident came to see me. Dad had gone home to get some clothes but Mum was still there. When they walked in, I must have recognised them because Mum said the left side of my face curled up in a sort of smile. This was the very first sign that I saw anything or recognised anyone. Everyone was pleased.

The youth worker in the hospital came to see me and encouraged Mum to take me down to the teenage room. I was put in my armchair and pushed (it was on wheels) out into the corridor and into the lift. There were some other teenagers there about my age and they played music to me and tried to talk to me. After about fifteen minutes I'd had enough and they rang up to the ward to tell them I was coming back.

I could only cope with so much at a time and this visit exhausted me so I was put back to bed. I spent more time in my chair every day though, but I still couldn't support my head or move much. I had a few more visitors whilst I was there including my Nan and Grandad but I can't recall whether I recognised them or not.

When my specialist came round to see me one day, he asked Mum and Dad about our local hospital and said he would find out if they would be able to cope with my special needs.

They were confident that they could and I was moved by ambulance at the end of May 1996. Mum travelled with me in the ambulance and Dad drove the car behind. We were all exhausted by the time we got there. I settled in and Mum stayed with me and was given a bed in another room.

Chapter 4

Please save our girl's life (1996)

By Katie's mum

On the day of the accident my husband, Bob, and I were both at work.

I received a phone call at my desk at Holland Training Centre where I worked as a Training and Recruitment Manager.

The call was from one of the students at the yard. She told me that Katie had been in an accident and an ambulance had been called. She said she had no more details but would keep me informed of where Katie was being taken. I telephoned Bob and then waited for more news.

After an hour I hadn't heard anything so decided to phone the yard again. This time the call was answered by the mother of one of Katie's friends. She told me that Katie was going to be taken by air ambulance to a hospital but they hadn't decided which hospital to go to yet.

By this time, we were frantic with worry and realised how serious it was. After an age of waiting, we were finally informed by the yard that she was going to the local Pilgrim Hospital in Boston. I telephoned Bob again and we met there. We were shown to a relative's room and joined by a doctor who explained Katie's injuries.

Katie had been resuscitated (CPR) twice and was now in a critical but stable condition. The results of the scan were faxed to Queen's Medical Centre in Nottingham and they confirmed that they would accept and treat her there. Once again, the Air ambulance was made ready and Katie was flown to Nottingham.

Bob and I made a quick stop at home to pick up a few things and drove immediately to Nottingham where we were able to see Katie for a few minutes before she was taken to theatre a little after 8pm on the 11 April.

Maria, the doctor's assistant, joined us for a few minutes and explained the situation. She pulled no punches and told us the worst scenario - Katie may not survive.

The depressed fracture had bruised the brain and there was a clot that had to be removed. It was a very delicate operation but they would do everything they could. We also saw the cosmetic surgeon who would sew on Katie's ear.

The waiting seemed endless. We sat and waited for hours before Katie finally returned to the ward at around 3pm the following day (12 April 1996). Maria came to see us again – "so far, so good" she said. After we had seen Katie again for a few minutes we were given a room and tried to get some sleep - it didn't come easy.

The next morning, we were at Katie's bedside very early to check on her condition. She had been put on a cool bed to keep her temperature and the pressure in her brain down. There also wires and tubes all over the place and a monitor with heart pulse and pressure rates.

After trying to eat breakfast we returned to the ward to see the neurosurgeon, Mr Punt.

He told us that the next 72 hours were critical and explained that the pressure in Katie's head must not rise above 30 as this would mean her brain was still swelling and could be deadly.

We watched that monitor constantly over the next few days. Once the pressure went to 32 and we got very upset, but the doctors rushed in and managed to get it back down.

We had visits from the family who encouraged us to get some fresh air and even go out to eat. Although we didn't want to, it helped to get away for a while. We both felt numb and dealt with this crisis in different ways. Whilst I was very quiet and didn't talk much, my husband, Bob, was constantly chatting. He talked about everything under the sun except Katie. It was his way of dealing with it.

On the day they decided to take the ventilator away I finally cracked and broke down. When I saw Katie struggling to breath on her own, I thought it was all over and ran from the ward. The ventilator was re-connected and they tried again after a few days. This time it was more successful and Katie could breathe on her own.

Our days were filled with sitting by Katie's bed - talking, reading to her and playing tapes of music she liked. I helped to wash her and did passive exercises with her limbs. She also had physio twice a day and her blood pressure, pulse, and temperature were checked every half hour. There was constant attention from both doctors and nurses.

I was very sceptical when they decided to move Katie to the neuro ward on 25 April. I hadn't looked or thought any further than one day at a time so being made to look ahead and suddenly realising what life was going to be like was another shock.

The move went ahead and Katie settled down in the neuro ward. The days carried on much the same but with the inclusion of a speech therapist trying to help Katie to swallow and the physios trying to get her out of bed and into a chair for part of the day.

As Katie still could not move or support her head she had to be propped up. By this time some of the tubes had been removed but there were nappies to change as well as washing and exercises to do.

Mr Punt, the neurosurgeon, appeared regularly and one day asked us where the nearest hospital to home was. He said a local hospital would be better for us all.

Again, we were shocked and horrified but realised that Katie's stay in hospital would be a long one and that we should think about it. Our local Pilgrim Hospital in Boston assured us they could cope with Katie's needs and we moved Katie there on the 9th May almost exactly four weeks on from the accident.

Chapter 5

A vulnerable little girl full of wires (1996)

By Katie's Auntie and Uncle

On the Thursday before Easter, I decided to phone my Brother as I hadn't spoken to him for about a month.

I lived in Hertfordshire and worked in Docklands at the time. I phoned him just after lunch and spoke to one of his work mates. He told me that my Brother was on his way to the local hospital as Katie had been airlifted there after having an accident.

I found the phone number of the local hospital and got through to A&E.

The nurse there was very kind. She confirmed that my Sister-In-Law was already at the hospital and put her on the phone.

She was clearly confused as she had no way of knowing how I knew about the accident. My Brother had not arrived at that stage and my Sister-In-Law naturally wanted to get off the phone to find out more about Katie. She promised to telephone me later that night once she knew more.

On Thursday night, my Sister-In-Law phoned to tell me that Katie had been airlifted to Queen's Medical Centre Hospital in Nottingham and they were waiting for an assessment.

We were on pre-booked break to Norfolk Broads that weekend but kept in constant touch with the hospital while we were away.

My Sister-In-Law told us that Katie was going to have an operation and that her chance of survival was one in three. It was a very long weekend. I didn't speak to my Brother much. He didn't want to put things into words because it would make it too real.

We were due to come back to London on the Monday morning and I had planned to see my Mum and Step Dad in the afternoon.

I spoke to my Brother to ask him if he had spoken to our parents and he said no. I thought this was a little short-sighted as my Brother always phoned our Mum on a Saturday, and she would worry if there was no answer on the phone.

I asked him what I should say to Mum. He suggested that I tell her that Katie had had an accident and had concussion. I think I said "don't be stupid, if I lie to Mum she'll never trust me again." Anyway, on the 8-mile drive from my house to Mum's I rehearsed what I was going to say.

When my Step Dad answered the door, he knew something was wrong. He followed me into the lounge and stood behind Mum's chair with his hands on her shoulders. I knelt in front of her and told her that Katie had had a riding accident, her chances of survival were slim and that she was still unconscious after her operation. It was the hardest thing I have ever had to do in my life.

Over the next few days, the whole family was in constant contact. My husband and I had arranged to go up to Nottingham the following weekend (7 days after the accident). The children were going to stay with their Grandparents. We booked into a motel close to the hospital.

I had spoken to the ward to ask if it would be appropriate for us to try to get my Brother and Sister-In-Law out of the hospital for a couple of hours. The sister said "yes please." There were things that needed to be done which would be better with parents out of the way.

When we arrived, we were taken in to a family room where the medics explained how Katie would look and what to expect. My Sister-In-Law had already told the hospital that I was prone to fainting. My Brother and Sister-In-Law looked as though they hadn't slept in a week. They looked grey and had lost weight. We had taken a bottle of scotch with us and they clearly needed it.

I did not expect what I saw. What you see in television programmes is nothing like the real thing. Although I didn't faint, I felt a bit dizzy. I saw a little girl, very vulnerable, very frail, full of wires, with monitors surrounding the bed. There was a large, what looked like a nut and bolt in her head. My Brother was fussing and talking almost non-stop, he always does this when he is worried. My Sister-In-Law just looked exhausted.

We stayed for about half an hour or so and then all went back to the motel for dinner.

A mobile phone which was in the middle of the table throughout the meal.

The following week was no better. Katie was taken off the coma inducing drugs and they were hoping that she would regain consciousness within the allotted time. Unfortunately, she didn't and it was very distressing. My Brother still hadn't spoken to our Mum, so she was phoning me every day getting more and more upset.

I had promised to take Mum and Step-Dad up to Nottingham on the Saturday or Sunday (I can't remember exactly which day) - which was two weeks after the accident. By this time Katie was out of intensive care and in a special ward. I phoned my Brother from the hospital car park to pre warn him as I knew that the situation was going to get emotional.

I wheeled Mum into the ward in her wheelchair with my Step Dad behind. We saw Katie sitting up in a special chair. She looked totally vacant, her eyes large pools of darkness, almost bottomless but nothing inside. She looked at the three of us without any expression. Mum was rushing words at her as if trying to get a reaction, Katie frowned, looking in her direction but not aware of who we were. We weren't there long before Katie was put back in to her special bed.

My children had both recorded a story on an audio tape in the hope that it may stimulate Katie. When my Son spoke, Katie looked confused and got restless. It occurred to me that the last time Katie had seen my children was at Christmas and since then his voice had broken, so she probably didn't recognise him at all. There was some recognition when she heard my Daughter's voice, but she didn't listen for long and was clearly becoming tired.

When it was time to leave, my Brother came down to the car to say goodbye to us all. It was then that he put his arms around Mum, broke down and sobbed. I explained to Mum on the way home that that was the reason he wouldn't speak to her on the phone was because he didn't want to cry. There were tears all the way home.

Chapter 6

Moved to a local hospital - a step closer to home (1996)

By Katie

On 4 May, 4 weeks after my accident, I was moved to the Pilgrim Hospital in Boston. I don't remember being moved but I do have some blurred memories.

I had my own room in the children's ward. It had a sink, drawers for clothes and TV with a video player. There was also a fold up bed for Mum or Dad.

One day I was on my own, as Mum had gone out, and I wanted to put a film on. I remember the film was Grease. The TV and video player were right in front of me, so I managed to get near the end of my bed and tried to put the video in. I couldn't reach it though and I fell on the floor. I couldn't stop laughing and thought it was funny! Mum came running to see what had happened and went to get a nurse to get me back on to the bed.

Another time, I had a few school friends over - Phil, Chris and Adam. It was kind of them to come but I think they were more interested in watching the football on the TV!

Then there was the time I managed to pull the feeding tube out from my nose and Sister Margaret had to come and put it back in. I was not amused and put up quite a struggle!

I always hated bath time because I had to sit on the swivel seat and be lowered into the bath. It made me dizzy but I wasn't able to express my feelings properly. I remember Mum and Sister Margaret trying to get me in and I managed to knee Sister Margaret and give her a black eye. Sorry Sister Margaret!

One day, two men came to see me. I was put in a wheelchair and we went downstairs to a big room that looked like a gym. With their help, I got out of the wheelchair. I put my hands on some bars and it helped me to walk. As I got better at walking I started on some stairs, there were only three going up and three going down but I managed okay.

When I got better at walking, I started walking to the school with my Mum next to me and my wheelchair behind me.

Chapter 7

Chocolate milk shake - Katie's first drink (1996)

By Katie's Mum

Once Katie had settled in at the Pilgrim Hospital, I started to play videos of her favourite programmes - one which was Neighbours - to see if there was any reaction.

The physiotherapist came to see Katie regularly and developed a programme to try and get her limbs working again.

It was slow work but eventually after many days they decided to put Katie on the tilt table.

This was a large table which she was put on flat and strapped in with special support for her knees. The table was then slowly tilted upwards so she was nearly in a standing position. At the start it was only for a couple of seconds and then gradually increased. One day they decided to put her feet on the floor but her knees collapsed.

The next day the physio brought another man with him, also a physio, who had a little more experience of Katie's type of problem. He asked the other physio to support her on one side whilst he took the other and gently lifted her off the bed. He wanted to see if there was any spontaneous reaction from her legs when she was lifted each side. Amazingly her legs tried to move - it was what they had hoped for.

Whilst this was taking place every day, Katie also had visits from Vicki who was the play leader. She was lovely and became a great friend.

She talked to Katie, joked and generally cheered her up.

Katie needed a lot of rest between these sessions but as the weeks went by, she was gradually able to stay awake longer.

Katie also started to have ten-minute visits from the school teacher. She would bring a keyboard to her bed to see if Katie could press any keys. After gaining a little bit more use in her arms, Katie was able to press a few keys and move her legs a little bit. It was all very slow but by the middle of June 1996 she could take a few steps and was able to press a few keys on the computer when the teacher came to see her.

Our next hurdle was getting Katie to eat. I tried to get her try some Weetabix but she didn't want to and it was chocolate milk shake that persuaded her to take her first taste of anything.

Gradually over 3 or 4 weeks she would eat a spoonful of jelly or mashed potato and her liquid food from the tube was reduced slightly. She had lost a lot of weight and the dietician came to her to plan her food intake both by tube and solids.

Katie settled down in to her routine and gradually began to take more and more steps. She also began to visit the school room for about half an hour at a time. One day Katie shouted at one of the teachers at school. She had become very upset with this particular teacher, and had complained about her quite a few times before. One day she said she didn't want to go back to the school but she did in the end.

The occupational therapist also visited to try and help Katie hold a spoon and get into the bath. By this time, Katie was being visited by physio, dietician, teachers, occupational and speech therapists as well as her doctor. All this was a lot for her, she was extremely tired and needed a rest between each therapy.

Little by little, Katie was improving though and after another meeting with the doctors, Bob and I decided to take the huge and terrifying step of taking her home for a weekend.

I just wanted a quiet weekend at home to get used the idea but Nana and Grandad were so desperate to see her that we agreed they could visit on the Sunday for a few hours.

Katie looked very pleased to be back in her room and in her own bed. Bob slept on the floor in her room in case she woke up in the night.

All in all, the weekend went well and Bob and I began to think we might be able to cope with Katie at home, once her feeding tube had been taken out.

Chapter 8

Katie comes home (1996)

By Katie's Mum

Eventually, after what seemed like forever, Sister Margaret arrived one morning to remove Katie's feeding tube. She could go come home at last but had to return to the Pilgrim Hospital for two hours schooling every day.

For the first few weeks, Bob slept on the floor in Katie's room while I got some rest.

Katie had to practice the stairs with the occupational therapist before she left hospital but it was still difficult for her doing it at home.

The days were filled with her daily visits back to the hospital and rest. This was all Katie could manage at first.

Bob and I thought it would be good to take Katie away for a few days. One of my Auntie's had a mobile caravan in Suffolk, so we went there for four days and had a lovely time.

There was a family staying opposite us with a couple of girls just a bit younger than Katie and she made friends with them. It made a nice change and cheered everyone up.

In September, Katie suddenly decided she wanted to go back to the stables. The very same stables where she had her accident. When we got there, they were all pleased to see her.

Bob and I arranged for her to sit on a very quiet pony to see what her reaction would be. His name was Edward and he belonged to one of the girls there.

Chapter 9

Riding again and epilepsy (1996)

By Katie

It was September 1996, five months after my accident, when I got back to the stables and on to a pony - and I instantly knew what to do.

I picked up the reins and put my feet in the stirrups the right way round without any prompting. I think everybody was surprised.

I had a short walk on him and then Dad lifted me off. After that, I went to ride Edward quite a few times and eventually I was able to ride my own pony, Ensign again.

When one of the girls got his tack out for me once, I instantly knew how to put the bridle and the saddle on. My Mum was in the stable with me at that time, but I managed to do most of it myself.

One day (14 September) I went to ride Ensign. When I got on, my head went down towards his mane very quickly. What I sat back up I started feeling dizzy. I think my eyes just went black because my head was so sensitive and it called an epileptic fit.

My Mum got me off Ensign and rang 999. When I woke up, all I could see was lots of people and doctors. They were talking about me having tablets because I had epilepsy.

I don't remember if we went back to that stables again, or what happened to Ensign, my pony.

I carried on with riding though but at a different riding school. There was a lady who had a quiet pony called Jacob. We tried him out and he was good so I rode him for a few months.

At this time, I was still attending my local Hospital School. I was taken there by a taxi. The lady was really nice, she used to walk with me up to the ward until eventually I felt ok going up and coming down myself. I still had to do my speech therapy and occupational therapy and various member of my family and friends from school came to see me.

I had a hearing test on Friday 4th October 1996 at the hospital because the school thought that I had a problem with my ears. They found that I had an infection in my left ear and some mites. The ear hadn't been cleaned out since the accident (6 months ago!) and the dirt and blood had caused an infection. It had to be washed out on a daily basis for two weeks and I didn't like it very much. After that I had to be very careful and a hearing test was arranged. I regularly visited Dr Crawford at the hospital in Nottingham, who looked after me during my stay there while I attended the hospital school.

Chapter 10

Back to school (1996/1997/1998)

By Katie

On 5th November 1996, seven months after my accident and now 14-years-old, I went back to my old school - Thomas Cowley School in Donnington.

I was really excited to go back to school and remember it was an art lesson in my year 9 class.

When it was lunch time all my friends took me to the Hall to get something to eat.

I don't think I could talk very much but I kept smiling after we sat down. Then the teacher from the local hospital came to collect me, which was quite upsetting.

I also remember trying to study French - goodness knows why I picked French, I couldn't even speak English properly!

Apparently, I went once a week for several weeks until Christmas in an effort to integrate back into main stream, but in the end I couldn't manage it and I had to carry on going to the local hospital school instead.

I started school at 9.30am and finished at 3.30 pm, so I was very tired when I came home, although I don't think I went every day.

I also had to go to speech and therapy sessions every Monday, Tuesday and Friday.

I started going to a group called Guides. It was fun and I made lots of friends.

The hospital told Mum and Dad about two boarding schools that specialised in speech therapy and suggested we visit them. I was a bit scared because they were so far away.

On 1 April 1997, just before my fifteenth birthday, we went to see both schools. The first school was in Derbyshire and I didn't like it but I liked the second school in Surrey called Moorhouse School & College. It was a long way away though and I would only be able to come home every two weeks. We decided to give it a test run and I went for two days in May. There's not much I can remember from those two days, apart from the fact that I got a boyfriend!

Moor House School

At Moor House, I was the only child who'd had an accident. All the other children had been born with some form of disability. Some used sign language although the majority could talk. The school was mixed, both boys and girls it was also primary and secondary school and was much more boys than girls.

I was struggling with my school work as I could not talk very well so I was kept in year 9 when I should have gone on to year 10.

This school was massive and had three floors. One the bottom we had classrooms, group rooms to go to after school, the hall, PE room, swimming pool, staff rooms, the nurse room where we had our medication and a huge dining room.

The second floor was more classrooms and one side was the boys' bedrooms. The third floor was girls' and boys' bedrooms.

There were other buildings where we went for speech therapy, and a building called Northanger where the secondary teenagers went after school.

Moor House was just like a normal school day. We were woken up every morning by a member of staff putting the lights on at 7.00 am - most of us were ready anyway to get to the showers first. I was lucky as my bed was near the showers.

After taking a shower we had breakfast in the huge dining room. We had to sit on our group tables, we couldn't go sit where we wanted. Each table also had a member of staff with us. While we were eating breakfast, we'd also choose our meals for the rest of the day.

When we had all finished our breakfast, one of us on the table had to take all the plates and cups to the kitchen. After that we would all go up to our rooms and brush our teeth, then go down to wait in twos to go in the hall for assembly. Then go to our classes.

When school had finished, we would go to our groups. Mine was Northanger. We had our own kitchen where we took turns each day making tea and toast for the others when school had finished. We had tables and chairs to sit and eat our snacks and two TV rooms - one for boys and the other for boys and girls. We had computers and a room with a stereo and (and lots of room to dance!) and a pool table.

Some of us would have swimming lessons after school. One day after I did a lot of swimming, I got out, had a shower and started feeling dizzy. My eyes went black and I had an epileptic fit.

I was lucky that the nurse room was near to the swimming pool. The fit was caused by chlorine in the pool, there was too much. From then on, I refused to go back in and got out of swimming sports day!

At 4 pm, we all had to go up to our rooms, do our homework and change out of our school uniform. At 5pm we went to a small room to get ready to go for dinner. At 9 pm we'd go to our groups. The girls would go up to their rooms and watch TV or just hang out. We had our own kitchen as well.

At 10 pm the lights went off. Most of the time the girls would stay up talking until the night staff came to check! The boys could stay in Northanger until 10 pm as they didn't have a TV or kitchen.

During year 9, I remember my Mum organising a charity horse show for the air ambulance that saved my life.

I had a table selling crafts that Mum and I had made. My friend Adam from Thomas Cowley School was there too. I also started riding for the Riding for the Disabled

Association (RDA). I rode a pony called Crystal and we started training for dressage shows. I also qualified for the RDA National Championships and rode another pony called Tom.

When I went back to school in September 1997, I was in year 10. My class had six boys and three girls (including me).

I remember Maths being way too hard for me. I couldn't understand it at all. I don't remember much about the English apart from reading. We had PE and did a lot of running.

We also had art, science, pottery and speech and therapy with different teachers. I always loved my art and did a lot of Picasso's art work with pastels. It sometimes got a bit messy! I also liked pottery, but that got a bit messy too!

Science was another subject in which I didn't have a clue. I remember falling asleep in the class once, although I don't think I got told off!

During class time, I had a support worker to help with my work. She was just there for me, not anyone else. First it was okay but I didn't like it after a while. The class was very small and the lady used to sit right behind me.

While I was trying to work, she was constantly asking if I was okay, which was very annoying. I couldn't get on or concentrate on my work and I couldn't wait for break time. It felt like I was being suffocated!

When I got a bit better with my speech and my work, she wasn't so bad but she was still sitting right behind me.

I didn't get on with the girls, but I did get on well with one boy who used to sit next to me in my class. He was only a friend though.

All girls were in sort of gangs. I think they picked on me as I had support worker and wasn't able to do the same work. They used to say some horrible things to me that upset me. I had that throughout year 10.

In 1998, I was in year 11. I was 16-years-old and the oldest in the class.

I was getting a lot better with my speaking and work so went to ask the Head Teacher if my support worker would not sit right behind me any more so she could help others in the class. It turned out to be a right nightmare as my support worker told all the boys and girls in the class, which was really embarrassing.

Also, as I the oldest in the class, I asked if I could miss the science lesson and do something else as I still had no idea what the teacher was talking about.

The Head Teacher agreed and they gave me some work experience to do, which was helping out at the local primary school.

It was great helping at the local primary school but the support worker coming used to come as well which was totally embarrassing - I felt like she was my shadow!

In the end, the Head Teacher agreed I could go by myself, which I did for the rest of the year. I really enjoyed spending my mornings at the primary school.

In year 11, I was still getting picked on. One day I was so upset I couldn't take anymore. I ran to the pay phone near where the science room was so nobody could see me.

I was crying when I rang my Mum and told her I wanted to come home. My Mum rang the school to tell them about the bullying. The girls who were bullying me were sent to the Nurse's room and told to stop doing it - but it just made the bullying worse and they carried on. Another time, I remember running upstairs to my bed and crying my eyes out. This time the girls were warned that they would be excluded if they carried on. It worked though. After that the bullying largely stopped.

When I had my 17th birthday, one of the members of staff who I'd always got on really well with, invited me to her house for dinner and to then watch a film. The head teacher said it was fine and I had a great time. I met her boyfriend and her little dog. I don't remember the name of the film but it was a big cinema.

Towards the end of year 11, I felt like things were getting better and I did some more work experience but in a different place. I don't remember the name of the place but it was like a big farm with a play area and café. Lots of children from different schools used to come and see the animals. My job was to look after the chickens and show them to groups of children. I did lots other jobs too. I cleaned up the rabbits and helped out with the horses and ponies. I also helped out in the café at some point. The work experience was only meant to be for two weeks but I ended up doing three weeks as I'd finished all my school work.

In year 11, each child left on a different date. It was very hard leaving as I was very close to my teacher and another member of staff. They were like a Mum and Dad to me. On my last day I was crying and looking back through the car window was heart breaking.

Chapter 11

College and working with children (1999)

By Katie

I enrolled at the College of West Anglia in Kings Lynn in 1999 for a course called "Introduction to Caring and Caring Services" (working with children).

Before I started college, I had to go and meet my teacher. I was told I would be in a class with people who had the same sort of problem. That made me feel totally thick. I just wanted to be normal.

I thought college would be better than school and I'd be more independent, but it wasn't. I still had to have someone helping me with my work and it made me feel useless.

I had to be picked up by a taxi every day as I couldn't (and wasn't allowed to) drive and it was too far for Mum and Dad to drive as they had to go to work.

I remember being really embarrassed on the first day. We stopped off on the way to college to pick up others who had a disability but we were dropped off at college next to all the normal people who were waiting to go in.

When I got out the taxi the lady who was going to help me came to me straight away and with a badge which was even worse. She sat right next to me in class. So much for being able to make friends!

When it came break time, I got up to go to get a drink and of course she came with me again! The same happened at lunch time.

As time went by, I felt her being with me all the time was really unnecessary. I'd made friends with normal people and even had a boyfriend. I'd go outside to hangout but this woman was like my shadow. I spoke to my teacher to say that she was not needed at break time or lunch time as I needed my own space.

My course included English, Maths, IT, Health & Safety and Food Hygiene while my work experience was at a nursery. The women who help came with me to the nursery as well but I soon sorted that.

Every Thursday we got on a bus to a big old building (I can't remember what it was called) and helped out with dinners for elderly people.

We had to take their money (so basically adding and taking away), get the tables ready, prepare the food, cook it, serve it and clean up after.

Apart from one girl, I didn't really get on with the people in my class. I ended up finishing the course at home rather than in college as I'd had enough of being in class. Everyone just seemed to fight about silly things like boyfriends and who was the cleverest. They were all older than me but acted like kids. I used to ignore them and got on with my work.

The course was only four days a week so on Friday I'd go to one of my Sister's friends as Mum was working. At weekends I used to go out clubbing with my friend Hannah. We always went to the pub first and then clubbing. There were lots of different clubs we went to and most of the time she had a lot of her friends with us. I never went home after clubbing, I always stayed over at her house then went home later in the day. Not much else I can remember about that really!

Chapter 12

My first job (2000)

By Katie

After college my mum found me a part time job at a residential home.

I walked there and back myself, which was good. I didn't have anyone else watching over me either, which was even better!

My job involved washing and the drying the clothes, taking the trolley round for a cup of tea and biscuits, getting lunch ready, serving and washing up.

It was alright for a while, until they started to make fun of me. I was getting very upset. I didn't understand why at first but now I think it was because I didn't always understand what they were saying because of my head injury. I'd often get confused and cry. I still do that now sometimes, being confused that is.

After I left the residential home, I tried various groups.

I joined a maths group for people with understanding problems but I didn't stay long as it said something about disability at the top of the entrance outside. I felt totally embarrassed and just wanted to be normal. I tried another group doing the same thing but didn't like it there either and left. To be honest, I don't think I wanted to go to either group in the first place. I just had to do what I was told, like being a child again.

Next, they found a group called Headway for people with head injury. I was taken there in a taxi and really liked it at first. It was just like messing about, playing games on a computer and chatting. At one point we had to move to a different place and everything changed. We were put in groups and had to write down in a diary what we had been doing each day. I didn't see the point of that and didn't want to do it. So I left in the end.

Around that time, I met a lad who worked with my Sister. He was a really nice person and ended up being my boyfriend.

One night, when we were walking into town for dinner, I started feeling dizzy and knew I was going to have an epileptic fit. I couldn't talk so turned around and started walking back the other way. I don't remember what happened next. When I woke up, I was in an ambulance on the way to hospital. The doctors came to see me to talk about increasing my medication to control my fits. After that my boyfriend didn't really talk to me much and didn't sit anywhere near me when he came to see me. We split up in the end, I could tell it would have something to do what had happened when I had a fit.

Towards the end of the year (November 2000) Mum found me a volunteering role at my local primary school. I helped in reception and really liked it so I stayed there.

Chapter 13

Support Workers (2001)

By Katie

Due to my accident, I needed support workers (or carers) all the time.

I wasn't allowed out on my own because of my epilepsy and, because of my head injury, people thought I couldn't manage on my own.

I didn't agree though, I thought I was fine!

Mum always said that I had to meet the support workers first to decide if I liked them or not. I didn't feel like I had much choice to be honest - I had to do what I was told.

In the meetings there would be me, Mum, and the support worker. I also had a case manager, a lady who managed all my care arrangements.

At the time, Mum and Dad were only working part time, as they didn't want me to be on my own.

What made things even worse was that the support workers were meant to wear a badge to show that I was disabled. I wouldn't let them wear it though. It was too embarrassing as I didn't look disabled. Most of the time people would think the support worker was my mum as I looked very young for my age.

I can remember some really bad experiences with support workers.

One particular lady I'll never forget. She was constantly asking if I was okay, and whether I wanted anything.

In the end, I went to my bedroom to be on my own. I put a film on and just sat on the bed.

She (the support worker) knocked on the bedroom door and asked if she could watch the film with me. I couldn't say no. In the end, I told the case manager about her and explained that I needed my own space.

Another time, I was in the car with a support worker. The car was very small and she wasn't a small lady, so it was a tight fit and I felt very closed in. I must have said something as she replied "don't worry" and put her hand on my knee / thigh. It really frightened me. Just imagine it happening to you.

On another occasion, I was at my Mum and Dad's bungalow. The phone rang and I answered it. When I picked the phone up, the man at the end of the line was asking me lots of questions and I just kept saying yes. At this point the support worker started listening to my conversation. As soon as she heard what the man was talking about, she blocked me off against the wall so I couldn't move. She pulled the phone off me and started having a go at me. It was really frightening. I didn't say anything about her as I was too scared.

Some of the support workers were okay though.

One of them was also a teacher who I did art and science with. I think the science was biology. I enjoyed it.

Another support worker, who was around the same age as me, used to take me to the pub to socialise with other people. I really enjoyed that too.

I'd also go out with one of my old friends from normal school. We'd go out every weekend to the pub first and then to a nightclub called Merlins.

I also went on holiday to a disability group in 2001. I wasn't happy about it at first. When we got there, I was told to sleep downstairs in a room for disabled people. Straightaway I said no - I wanted to sleep upstairs. I felt like I was being treated differently to everyone else. I hated that feeling.

One of the activities on that holiday was climbing - but I didn't do it as I was scared about having an epileptic fit. Night time was a lot of fun though! We had a pub to go to and there was a nice lad who used to serve drinks. He wasn't disabled, he just worked at the pub. I don't think he was really interested in me though.

I'll never forget getting up and singing in front of everyone one night. I was probably totally rubbish but I didn't really care then! On the last night we had a dinner and then a disco.

I really enjoyed singing. I used to sing at home too so I decided to have some lessons. My support worker would take me there, wait in the car (that I did not like) while I had my singing lesson and then we'd go home together. I didn't keep the lessons going for very long. They tried to teach me Opera and it was too hard!

During 2001, I was told to start looking for a house to rent. In the end, we found a house not too far from Mum and Dad's.

The house needed decorating as I didn't like the colour. It was empty as well so we had to look for new furniture. Eventually when we had everything we needed, I started sleeping at my new, rented house for a few nights a week.

It was a big change for me. I was used to sleeping at the bungalow with everyone on the same level so I wanted the support worker to come upstairs with me at the start.

At first, I couldn't sleep well as the rented house had a double bed and I was used to a single. To make things better, we changed the beds over using the trailer we used for the horse shows.

Talking of horses, I was still enjoying riding and competing with the Riding for the Disabled Association (RDA). I can remember riding a pony called Rosie - I can't remember where we finished though.

In the middle of the year, I got my own pony, a 13tt Hand Chestnut, Cob. He was a lovely pony called Sam and we got on really well. I think Cobs are the best ponies as they are very clever and they understand you. My Mum and Sister also had a horse called Jack and we used to go out show jumping most weekends.

Sam never put a pole down but I fell off sometimes - most of the time in a double jump or if Sam put an extra stride in.

At the weekend, a lorry driver used to the come to the yard with cheap cigarettes from abroad.

One time, after I said hi, he asked me out. My Mum and Dad were not keen on him but I still went out with him anyway!

On the swing wemade

With Daniel at the Farmhouse

At the Farmhouse

At home playing golf

At Thomas Cowley Sports Day

At home after leaving hospital. Dad and Nan behind me

At home after leaving hospital

At boarding school

At boarding school

My 21st Birthday

With Hannah who used to live near our farmhouse

Ready to go clubbing with Lucy

With Adam from Thomas Cowley School at a charity horse show for Air
Ambulance

Ruby and Jasmin

Me on Barney

Barney jumping at the livery yard

Ensign

Me, Ensign and mum

Me, mum and Ensign

Me, mum and Ensign

The pony I saw when I stopped seeing Ensign

Sam

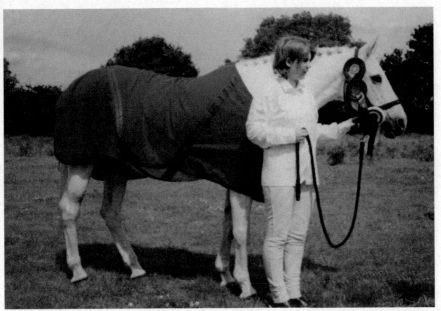
Crystal, RDA winner, championship

Tom

Riding Rupert doing my test

Breezer

Me and Rufus at the championships we won

Rosie

Me and Freddie

Tommy

Tommy

With my mum

Chapter 14

My new (care) home (2002)

By Katie

I enjoyed getting my own place and it was exciting to decorate.

What I didn't like was being with support workers all the time! It felt like I'd moved into a care home rather than my own home. It was like having a full-time babysitter.

A lot of the time I'd go up to my bedroom as I wanted to be on my own. I used to go up to bed early and watch TV so there was no need to be with the support worker.

I also didn't like the fact that the support workers kept writing down all the things I was doing during the day. I didn't see the point of this, or why they did it. I thought they were being nosey.

Around this time, I also started meeting with these people called solicitors. They kept asking me all sorts of questions about my accident and how I was coping. I didn't know all the answers and it upset me and made me cry. They needed to know what I could and couldn't do and how many support workers I needed as there was going to be a court case to decide how much money I would need for the rest of my life.

I was still volunteering at primary school until July 2002, but it was getting harder for me to help with the school work as I was going to different classes in different years. In the end, I found another paid job cleaning at an old primary school which had been turned into a community hub were they would do all sorts of things like art to yoga. I was working separately as a cleaner as well. I only stayed for about two months though as the other lady kept asking me to work at weekends, which I couldn't do as we went show jumping every weekend.

My passion for horses was as strong as ever and I rode another lovely horse for the RDA called Rupert. We qualified for the championships and won.

I was still with my boyfriend I met at the stables at this point and he came to the championships. I can't remember if he watched but I remember I left with him before the results were announced. My Mum and Dad were not pleased as I wasn't there to collect the trophy. Thankfully my teacher sorted things out and I got the trophy in the post.

As I'd stopped volunteering at the primary school my mum found me a pre-school called Stepping Stones to volunteer at.

The staff at Stepping Stones could understand a bit more about what I could and couldn't do. For example, if I didn't feel very well or I had a bad headache, which was quite a lot of the time, Mum or the support worker would ring them and let them know I wouldn't be coming in. They always understood. There were plenty of staff there so it wasn't a problem.

Chapter 15

Being made to finish with my boyfriend (2003)

By Katie

In 2003, we sold Sam (and Jack) - and for a while I didn't have my own pony.

I decided I'd really like an Appaloosa (an American horse breed best known for its colourful spotted coat pattern) so we went to an auction.

We had a look round at the horses and ponies and there were two in particular that I liked. There was an older horse who was good at everything and a younger one who needed to be schooled. I picked the younger one and we took him straight home in our trailer after Dad successfully bid for him.

I called my new Appaloosa, Freddie. At first, we didn't do any riding as he was only two years old, and you're only supposed to start schooling horses when they're around four. To be honest, he was a bit of a handful so my Sister ended up having him.

At some point we moved to a different Livery Yard, nearer to where I lived. There were a lot more people around my age there. As I couldn't ride Freddie, we looked for another pony and found a 14.2 Bay Thoroughbred called Tom.

Tom was fine when I rode him where he lived but as soon as we brought him to the Livery Yard, he just wasn't the same. We kept him for a while to see if he would change but, in the end, we had to sell him.

We still had Freddie and I was helping by grooming him and tacking him up. As my sister had started riding him, and he seemed okay, I got on him once. I was very nervous and Freddie picked that up. He started fidgeting so I got off straight away.

There was another pony and the stables called William. He was a lovely pony and the owner said I can ride him until I found my own.

I was still riding with the RDA and qualified for the championships again with Rupert. This time I stayed to see the results and I won again.

At this time, I split up with my boyfriend. We then got back together but nobody knew. We soon split up again though. I'll tell you why.

One night he was waiting for me outside my house in his car. I told the support worker I was going outside to see a friend. The next morning the support worker who shouted at me about the phone call was working. When the night support worker had gone, she went to look at the folder and read that I had gone outside to see a friend. She worked it out straight away and knew I'd gone to see my boyfriend. I was in the dining room at this point and she came in and told me very loud, like an adult would tell off a child, "that wasn't a friend you went out to see, I know it would be your boyfriend. You finish with your boyfriend or I will tell your parents."

I was terrified and started crying. I had to text my boyfriend and finish with him. She should never have made me do that.

Another time, I went into town one day and we were walking past a tattoo shop. I decided I wanted a tattoo and picked a devil for my ankle. The shop had to ask for ID to prove my age! When this nasty support worker found out about the tattoo, she went absolutely nuts!

Chapter 16

What's the point of staying alive? (2004)

By Katie

I only kept a diary for 3 months of 2004 - but it's long enough to see that I had lots more experiences, good and bad, with support workers!

One of them was a friend of the support worker who shouted at me about my tattoo and made me finish with my boyfriend - but I got on a lot better with her.

Her name was Beverley and she worked every Monday and Tuesday. On Monday, we'd normally go into town. We used to go to an antique shop or another shop called 'Flowers and Things'. I'd always end up buying something as I like my nick-nacks. After shopping, we'd go off for lunch at a café. Then I'd go home for a rest.

On Tuesday, we'd go to the Sports Centre and play Badminton for about an hour. It was hard at first although I think it would be hard for anyone who'd never done it before. The next day my arm was always aching too!

One day after we played badminton we went to the cafe. As I drank my hot chocolate I started laughing as one of us must off said something funny. The drink went down the wrong way and I ended up choking. The next thing I remember is waking up in the back of an ambulance.

I can remember two support workers who became more like friends really. Both of them had horses and one was a riding teacher as well. They'd take me out at night and generally gave me a lot more space.

There was another support worker who just took no notice of what I wanted to do. She never stopped talking and it was too much for me. One time, she took me to a farm type place. When we paid to get in, I was put through as a child. I was 21 at the time and I wasn't happy with the support worker for not saying anything.

Another time she was planning to take me to London. I thought it would be great until she said that another support worker was coming too. I asked her why and she said because London was a big place. Both the support workers were really tall and they stood on either side of me. It felt so claustrophobic.

In 2004, I also started a Young Farmers Group. I was nervous at first meeting new people but I ended up making new friends. What I didn't want, was the support worker coming with me all the time!

One day, I told the support worker I wanted to go to the Young Farmers Group with one of my friends instead of her. The case manager wouldn't allow it though and in the end my friend didn't want to come with me. It upset me. I still went with the support worker though.

After we had been looking for a while, we eventually found another horse. Rocky was a 15.2 Bay Thoroughbred and he was a dressage horse. I rode him quite a few times at the owner's place first before we brought him home.

When he arrived at the yard everything was okay to begin with but we soon had exactly the same problems we had with Tom. It was very upsetting.

One time we took Rocky to Sheepgate Riding School in Boston for a dressage show - but it didn't go well. He kept going into a canter when it was supposed to be a trot.

On the way home from the show, the trailer kept moving as Rocky wouldn't stay still. We were worried he might have fallen over. We found somewhere to stop and saw that he was sweating and shaking really badly.

When we got him home, he was still sweating and barged out of the trailer.

Unfortunately, our problems with Rocky didn't end there. As time went on, he kept biting the other horses in the paddock and the owner of the yard said we couldn't keep him there anymore.

We tried moving Rocky to another yard to sell him but he started causing problems there too so we had to bring him back. Eventually, we split the paddock so he could be on his own. I don't know why they didn't do that in the first place. But the owner of the yard still didn't want him.

This is what I wrote in my diary at the time:

"I couldn't sleep very well that night, I was crying most of the night. I thought what is the point of staying alive, I did because of Rocky but now he has to go back, I haven't got a boyfriend, I feel lonely, I have so many people working for me, they drive me round the bend. I have another bloody year 'til the court is done and I've been told I can't have the type of house I want with stables. I can't get married, so I don't really want to stay alive, I just don't think I've got the guts to take all my tablets. I don't know what they will do, but what is the point of staying alive?"

I just didn't feel like my life was worth living.

I started riding William again and we took him and Freddie to Sheepgate. I did a lot of showing and won a class so I qualified for the championships. I won the family pony, 2cd best ridden and 4th best suited.

By October (2004), we still couldn't sell Rocky, so we made the decision to go to Overa Farm Stud in Kings Lynn, to swap him for another horse.

We looked at two horses. The first horse was called Charlie. My Sister got on and then me - but he wasn't right for us. The second horse was a mare called Heidi. She was a flea-bitten grey 17hh Dutch Warmblood. She was perfect so we swapped her for Rocky.

It was heart-breaking to watch Rocky go - he didn't want to get in the horse box and I felt terrible. Horses are very clever - they know what is happening and he looked terrified.

I decided to change Heidi's name to Breezer.

In December, I got a phone call from my Mum saying that Breezer hadn't been well. She wouldn't eat all her dinner and was rolling in her stable. In the end, we called the vet and she was diagnosed with colic. Although she got better, the same happened on Christmas Eve.

She recovered again but on 29th December, I got another call from my Mum saying Breezer wouldn't get up and hadn't eaten her breakfast. I got to the stables straight away and she was standing up but it didn't take long before she was lying down again, then up again.

At that point, we called the vet again. While we waited, we got her out of her stable and took her in the school to keep her walking rather than lying down or rolling. When the vet arrived she said she had got colic again and was treated.

I got another call from mum saying Breezer wouldn't get up or eat her breakfast again. I went to the stables straight away and we called the vet. Breezer got better again but something wasn't right…

Chapter 17

I couldn't say goodbye (2005)

By Katie

On 26th January (2005) I was sitting upstairs in my computer room at home when Mum arrived. I could see in her eyes that something had happened with Breezer. Tragically, she had passed away in the horsebox on the way to the vets.

There are lots of different types of colic for horses. I think the worst part is horses can't be sick and if they can't go to the toilet that's it. With Breezer her guts got twisted which is why she couldn't survive.

I was so upset but after Mum told me, she just went home. I was crying the whole time and didn't want to be on my own. I just felt totally lost.

This is what I wrote on my diary that night

'I am lost at the moment, it feels like a fantasy dream and will be alright next day, but it won't she can't come back never I have to face to it every morning'.

After Breezer passed away, everyone from the stables gave us flowers and a card which was nice. My Mum and Sister still had to go to the stables as we had Freddie. Mum would always keep her emotions to herself that's how mum handles it.

At first, I found it too upsetting to go to the stables but eventually I started riding William again.

In March 2005, we started looking for a different Livery Yard. I don't remember why but the one we found was much better. It was a massive big warehouse turned in to stables. It had lots of acres, with a cross-country and a proper set of show jumping jumps. Although the yard wasn't quite ready, so we put our name down.

As a stop-gap, we moved to another yard just down the road. I carried on riding William and also did some freestyle with Freddie. I lunged him at first, leading him a circle around the enclosure then, when I took the lunging line off, he copied whatever I did. It was fun!

Reading through my diaries, I can see that on the 24 March 2005, we started looking for another horse. One of the horses we looked at was a mare 15.1hh. It was a cross Arab. God only knows why we went to see this horse. I would never pick an Arab. It was lame. So that was a no no.

The next one we looked at was a horse in Sheepgate. It also was a mare, 16.2hh Dutch Warmblood, and very friendly. She stood still being tacked up but was very stiff when she was ridden.

In April, we went to see another horse in Sheepgate, as Mum knew the owner. It was a 16hh gelding, TB-Appaloosa high dressage. His name was Frankie and he was very friendly.

I went back to the stables at Sheepgate quite a few times with lessons just to make sure he was right one. One weekend at Sheepgate they were doing a show so we thought we'd have a go and if everything went okay we'd bring him home that day as well.

When we got there, Mum got on Frankie first and he went mad, picking up all four legs. My Dad and my Sister's boyfriend were there as well and they had to get hold of Frankie so Mum could get off. My Dad told me Mum actually fell off not got off!

When we got him back to the stables Frankie seemed fine, but he bit my Dad and my Sister's boyfriend twice. I was really upset it had all gone wrong. I was crying all the way back to the yard. Everyone was waiting to see my new horse and I just didn't know what to say.

I wrote this in my diary:

'I cry again, see solicitors, people with me all the time, not got my own house yet, bits being changed, I have to go to the RDA show. When I get a horse and my house I will get my life back, but at the moment I am depressed'

In the end I went to the RDA in May and actually won the dressage competition at Arena UK riding a lovely pony called Rufus. I got 70% in the first test and 66% in the second, winning both times and qualifying for the championships. I didn't compete in the end though as a lot had happened that year having lost Breezer and all the problems with Frankie.

Eventually, we found another horse called Laddie. He was a 16hh thoroughbred, dressage horse. When we went to see Laddie, I got on really well with him. I kept coming back to ride him and have lessons, just to make sure he was the right one. On the 4 June 2005 Laddie arrived to the stables (we had moved to the new indoor stables by then and all my other friends had come as well).

Everything was going okay until one day when I got Laddie out of the paddock. As we went past the gate he saw a tractor. He got a lot stronger and faster and wouldn't stand still when I got to open the next gate.

When I got him on the way to the yard he was still strong. I took him to the stables as we thought he might want a wee, but we were wrong.

Mum tacked him up and he still wouldn't stand still. I didn't want to ride him so Mum lunged him and he was still very strong. As time went on, he'd be good one day and naughty the next - so some days I'd ride him and some days I wouldn't. So my Sister ended up riding him as well as Freddie.

We spoke to Laddie's previous owner who said he was just strong and wouldn't take him back.

I rode Laddie at a dressage show but it didn't go well. He was naughty and kept bucking, and we finished 6th. In the end we had no choice but to put Laddie up for sale.

I was still carrying on with the Young Farmers Group in 2005 as well.

Eventually, the case manager agreed I could go to the Group with my friend and not the support worker.

One time, when I was playing pool, one of the lads asked me which school I went to. When I told him I'd left school six years ago you should have seen the look on his face!

I met a really nice lad one night and we swapped numbers.

The next day I sent a text but didn't get a reply, so I sent him another text.

This time he did reply, with this message:

"Sorry I'm kind of seeing someone else and don't think it be fair if I came round. Had a great night on Wednesday and really sorry to have given you the wrong impression, hope you ok."

My reply back was pretty blunt. I said:

"You horrible person. You used me you gave me all the signals. I don't think I'll speak to you again. I hate you!"

He didn't text me back after that!

Looking back, I was really lonely. Here's an entry from my diary from around that time:

"I haven't got my house, horse, my life. I haven't got a boyfriend, children or friends. I will be 23 this year and I am on still on my own."

Although I was becoming more independent there were some things I couldn't do.

I struggled with cooking as it was difficult for me to do more than one thing at the same time, like a roast. I also didn't like to be on my own at night. When the rota become messy and a support worker wasn't able to stay with me at night, I'd go to my Mum and Dad's instead.

Thankfully in 2005, the court ruled that I could get my own house and I moved in on 19 June.

It was an exciting time, but there were a lot of things that needed sorting in my new house.

In the garden, I needed a fence putting up. There were also a lot trees falling over, so we needed a gardener to cut and dig them out.

Inside, I chose blue carpet wallpaper with blue shapes. I don't think we had any other room decorated.

Although I'd moved to my new house, I was still having the same issues with support workers.

When I got home one day before 5 pm, the night support worker had already let herself in!

I wasn't happy. It was my house and she hadn't asked. Even my Mum and Dad used to knock on the door, but the support workers just used to let themselves in.

I'd thought it would be better living in my own house rather than a rented property but it wasn't. The support workers wouldn't give me any space at all. They were there all the time. I felt like I was suffocating.

I remember one time the support worker took me to the stables to meet up my Mum and Dad. I asked her to please to stay in the car as it was embarrassing for me. There were a lot of other people at the stables as well so I would feel claustrophobic.

She did get out of the car though and when I asked her why she replied 'I must get out of the car and do my job'. Everyone at the stables were watching and pointing. I was very upset and felt like I'd had enough - but there was nothing I could do about it.

The one good thing about getting my own house was being able to get my own cat.

On 23 July, I got two, 10-month-old kittens. I called them Ruby and Jasmin. Mum had only wanted me to get one kitten but they were just too sweet, I couldn't split them up!

The new house already had a cat flap, although it took them a while to get used to it. They were also naughty and did a lot of scratching! I can also remember the neighbour's cat coming into the garden and having a good hiss!

One day, Rosie got very ill, so I took her to the vets. It turned out that she'd eaten something poisonous. After a few more trips to the vets, they had to put her to sleep right in front of me. It was heart-breaking.

As time went by, I found the case manager was also getting more and more nosy. She'd question me about how I was spending my money and about going out to nightclubs. She also asked me what I was going to do if I met someone. I thought the questions were too personal.

I was continuing to have set-backs with my health too.

I also ended up in tears when we had a meeting (that I didn't want to go to) in the pub one time. I left early and wrote this in my diary:

"I cried, cried and cried but I don't know why. I have a house, I have a horse and it is nearly Christmas but I am so unhappy. I think there is just too much on, too many people around me. I have felt very, very locked in today with three support workers and me and I can't stand it".

Chapter 18

Court case settles (2006)

By Katie

By 2006 I had a new pony, Tommy. He was a 14.2hh Skewbald Cob and he was lovely.

When we went to see him, he was carrying a lot of weight and wasn't fit at all. Everything else was okay though, so I bought him with my savings.

On the day he arrived, we had everything ready and a few friends were waiting to see what he looked like.

The vet gave him a good check over too. He hadn't been wormed so that was sorted. His teeth looked terrible as well and needed to be done. He also needed the farrier (a specialist in equine hoof care) which he didn't like either!

We found out Tommy was between 4 and 5 years old when we had been told he was 6.

When I brought Tommy out or in, I noticed he leaned towards me and nearly put his foot on me once. He needed a lot of training and it took a while. He was a bit strong as well - bringing him in and out was hard work!

Tommy was fine being tacked up and groomed apart from when it came to his feet. He was very stubborn and wouldn't pick his feet up. He knew exactly what he was doing and was just playing a game. He also used to give us a present when we either combed his tail or cleaned his bum. He'd fart and the smell was terrible!

When we got to the point of clipping Tommy, he wouldn't stand still. Luckily one of the support workers, who was also my riding teacher, did the clipping for me. I don't remember how long it took, but it would have been a long time! After being clipped he'd have a long roll in the paddock so it must have made him very itchy.

Tommy was a lot lighter and easier to ride after being clipped but he still wasn't fit so we worked slowly. He'd also continue to play games when I went to get him. Sometimes he'd come to the front gate for me, but other times I'd have to go and catch him!

I brought him in once and he spooked at something but I managed to keep hold of him.

All in all, it was a lot of new things to learn. For example, when we got him in from the paddock and he had mucky fetlocks and shoes he'd need to be hosed before going in his stable. Tommy didn't like it, it would make his fetlock ticklish so when we used a sweat scraper to get all the water off he wouldn't stay still and started kicking!!

When I rode Tommy, I was constantly pushing him not kicking him to get him going as I didn't want him to get a dead leg. To help, I started using a wipe and spur but I only used it every so often. He needed a lot of teaching to get him 'under the bit' but we got there together and I was able to take him show jumping.

On 7 October 2016, the court case finally finished. The financial settlement my solicitors secured was enough to cover my care and living costs for the rest of my life.

When the case had finished, it was all over the newspaper and TV.

I was interviewed by the reporter for about an hour (I couldn't stop giggling for some reason at first!) and it ended up as a 5-minute slot on TV.

When my Mum spoke to the reporters she was like a different person. She spoke very seriously and in a different voice. It was almost like the case manager talking, not my Mum. It was difficult at the time as I didn't want my Mum getting too involved.

I wrote in my diary at the time:

"I thought it was good that it finished, but it wasn't it got a hell of a lot worse."

As I was in the newspapers and TV, I hated going outside. I'd wear a jumper with a hoodie by way of a disguise for a few weeks. Nobody asked me when I went into town but people talked about it at the stables and I didn't like it.

Nothing changed with the support workers at first either. I had a different case manager at this point and she told the support workers that they wouldn't be needed eventually as it was important for me to become more independent.

One particular support worker said, "but I need this job", which was silly as everyone knew I needed to work towards my independence. From then on, she was grumpy and snappy with me. When I changed the rota one week, the first thing she said was "am I still going to get paid?" In the end, I told the case manager and she left - but not without a fight!

One day, I asked one of the support workers about having a dog.

I'd always wanted a dog even though I still had my cat, Jasmin. I went to a shelter and found a dog I fell in love with straight away. He was a big dog, the size of a Great Dane but the build of a Labrador.

When we got him home, he settled in well. We had no issues with him going to the toilet, but he had an ear infection and needed ear drops so one of support workers took him home to look after him.

When Bev (support worker) arrived in the morning she asked where the dog was so I told her what had happened. Bev said she was happy to help if I got the dog back home so I did, although the other support worker wasn't happy.

We weren't allowed to take dogs to the stables, so Mum or Dad would have to look after him at their place which they didn't like.

The weekend I got my dog, there was a fair and Mum had a table selling crafts. I took the dog along, but Mum wasn't pleased. I don't know why but I was crying. Maybe I was a bit overwhelmed about the dog so I ended up calling the support worker (who looked after him when he had an ear infection) and she had him - which I something I regret.

I didn't know this at the time but apparently the support worker who took the dog said he'd damaged Mum and Dad's garage and a few other things.

Later in the year, I got another dog with Bev (the support worker I got on with). My new dog was a mix, part spaniel and he/she (can't remember) was very lively! I took the dog for a two hour walk to wear her it out but it didn't work – he/she was still going lively! In the end, Bev ended up taking this dog.

As the year went on, I was becoming more independent. A few of the support workers who helped during the day left as they weren't needed any more. I still had a few support workers at night as I wasn't used to being on my own.

As I had time on my hands, I started to volunteer at a charity shop called 'Lincolnshire Air Ambulance' – the air ambulance that saved my life. I only stayed for a few months though as around November I applied for a job at the new Homebase in town.

Lots of people applied to Homebase as it was a new shop with lots of different roles. When I went for the interview, Mum wanted the support worker to come with me. I wouldn't let the support worker come with me though - with so many people there it would just have been too embarrassing.

Without telling me, Mum told the support worker to tell the person doing the interviews that I had a head injury and sometimes struggled to understand things.

I didn't find out about this until later and I was very upset about it. I didn't agree with it either, I wasn't as bad as I had been.

The interview itself didn't take long and seemed to go okay. It was then just a case of waiting for the phone to ring to find out if I'd got the job.

It was very nerve wracking but I picked up the phone one day (my heart was pumping) and they offered me the job! I said yes!

Chapter 19

Working and dating (2007)

By Katie

Before starting at Homebase, I had to go on a training course. I can't remember if it was a 1 or 2-day course.

The course mainly covered health and safety and we were given a training folder.

We were also put into a group, given products and asked to show how we'd sell them to the public.

To finish off, we were put into another group to talk about helping customers by smiling, listening and being friendly.

I went to the training sessions on my own as I didn't want the support worker embarrassing me. After the initial training session, we had another three-week training programme at Homebase in Peterborough before our local store opened.

The support worker offered to give me a lift to Peterborough but I said no and found some other people to go with. When I started at Homebase where I live I went to and back in a taxi. The taxis were very unreliable though. I lot of the time they were either late or not turn up.

My job was Garden Assistant and involved watering the flowers, tidying up and monitoring the stock. I'd keep an eye on the flowers and replace them if necessary. When I'd finished, I'd take all the rubbish to the warehouse and throw all the old flowers away.

I did two mornings per week at Homebase which was enough for me. One time, I remember us all being shown how to use the paint machine, but it went in one ear and out of the other so I kept out of that!

Sometimes I was given other jobs, such as walking round the shop to see if any of the customers needed help. I can remember freezing after a few customers asked me questions and saying something like "I am really sorry, let me get another member of staff for you". Some customers were okay about it and others weren't.

It was always really hard to look for another member of staff anyway as lots of people were leaving because of the low wages!

I continued to have health issues while working at Homebase. Once, when I was washing the bottom of the metal shelves with a sponge, I had to stand up then go down on my knees to clean, then back up again, then down again. It made me feel dizzy and I couldn't carry on. I'm not sure if I told another member of staff or it was just the end of my shift.

It wasn't long before a lot of the friends I'd made started leaving Homebase and, to be honest, I didn't have a lot to do.

I decided I wanted to leave so I told them I had another job to go to (not that I did). Although there was a notice period of one month, they said I could leave straight away. I thought it was a bit rude really, they didn't even ask when I was started my new job!

One evening I got a call from the support worker. She said that she couldn't work that night, so I'd have to stay at my Mum and Dad's. I knew how unreliable the taxis were and really couldn't be bothered so I decided to stay at home on my own that night for the very first time.

I can't remember how I slept, but it must have been okay as I started to spend a lot more nights on my own.

As I was spending a lot of time on own, I registering with an online dating service to meet someone nice. I met some nice lads online but I was let down a lot. I met up with a few but didn't find the right lad for me.

Julie, who was a friend of my Sister's, started working with me at this time. Julie was the only one doing nights with Beverly doing the day. Julie and I used to go out every Monday to the sports centre, Tuesday dancing for two hours and Thursday clubbing - and this when I met someone.

He used to work during the week then come back to mine at the weekend and we'd go clubbing. We had a good time going out clubbing but I didn't like the fact that he used to drink and drive.

I was with him at Christmas 2007 but it wasn't the best. We went into town as I needed to buy a card. We ended up in "Shooters Bar" and he was drinking a lot of alcohol. He knew about my brain injury and I told him I wanted to go home and rest before we went out that evening. When I woke up after my rest, he was still out drinking. I sent him a text message and called but he didn't reply or pick up the call. I was really upset as I was looking forward to going out on Christmas Eve. Later that night he sent me some horrible text messages. I can't remember exactly what they said, but it was about us breaking up. Then, later on in the night, he called me saying it was his friend who had sent the horrible text messages, not him. He didn't even come home.

I thought straight away, "that's it, we're finished". I went upstairs, put all his clothes in a bin bag and left it at the front of the door. He eventually came home well past midnight and I pointed to the other room as there was no way he was sleeping with me. In the morning he went downstairs, saw all his stuff and just went without saying anything at all.

Chapter 20

Coercive control (2008)

By Katie

Despite what had happened with my ex-boyfriend, I carried on having nights out with Julie and her friends. One night we went to a pub and Julie noticed that was my ex was standing right next to me. I wasn't going to leave and ruin my night just because he was there though!

Nearly everywhere we went that night, my ex seemed to be there, hanging around like a bad smell.

When we got to the club, I started talking to some lads I knew.

They were standing right next to my ex so I swapped numbers with one of the lads (I wrote in my diary at the time that I wanted to rub my ex's nose in it!).

I ended up going to this lad's house for dinner. He lived with his parents and was a lot younger than me. The next day he sent me a text saying: "Sorry I can't do this, I can't do relationships". I was hurt and upset. I felt like I'd been used.

I still wanted to work so started volunteering at a charity shop called Sense, which supported the deaf and blind. I did Thursday and Friday mornings and I really enjoyed my job. I used to arrange, iron and price the clothes but I didn't use the till as it was too hard for me.

Although I enjoyed working at Sense, I left in the end. One morning I was late for work (probably because of the taxi). The manager must have got out of bed the wrong side that morning as she shouted at me even though I was only a volunteer. It made me really upset.

Towards the end of the year, I decided to give online dating another go so I signed up to a website called Plenty of Fish. I started chatting to a lad who sounded nice. He only lived 45 minutes away. Although it was a bit quick, we arranged to meet in a local pub. During the date, I told him about my accident. Actually, I ended up telling him far too much.

As usual, I was let down by the taxi coming home so the lad gave me a lift home. After that, we were an item and I went to his place at the weekend. Our Saturday night routine was to meet his friends and get a takeaway. I also met his parents.

There was one weekend when we had a party. It went on until 11 pm (or maybe later) and, at this point, there was only one of his friends still there. I was really tired so said something like "I'm knackered, I'm going to bed" to my boyfriend. He shot back "no you're not". He'd never spoken to me before like that and I looked at his friend. We were both shocked. I was scared of him after that.

Despite the incident at the party, I stayed with my boyfriend.

He was becoming more and more possessive though and was constantly texting me day and night. When I was with him, he was short tempered and controlling as well.

One weekend, I went to his friend's house for a takeaway. The girls and I went to get the food this time and we went to a supermarket to get some extra bits. The girls suggested I get something for my boyfriend. I wasn't sure at first but in the end I did. When we got back to their place, we got the food out and I gave my boyfriend the biscuit I'd bought for him. The first thing he said very sharply was "I don't want that" and he threw it back at me.

His attitude towards me got even worse as time went on. If I didn't get the food he liked, he'd go mad. I ended up terrified of him.

Towards the end of the year, Julie left as he put his place up for rent and moved in with me. Looking back, I really regret letting it happen.

When my boyfriend moved in, he brought his bed and bedroom furniture with him. He also brought his dining table and chairs with him. Oh, and his fish tank too.

The rest of the house was changed to how he wanted it. Instead of a nice wooden table and cream sofa in my TV room, he changed it to a black sofa, chairs and glass table.

Everything else in my TV room was either sold or given away to friends.

He also changed my bedroom with new furniture.

The spare room had always been a mess with all my school art work and other bits in it and he started having a go at me for not tidying it up.

He'd want to spend the weekend at his parents (he was a right mummy's boy) but he'd get cross if I wanted to see my family. In the end, I had to ask my mum not to text me if I was with him.

When he came home from work at night, he'd sit down straight away and either watch TV / his laptop or call his mum.

He'd tell me off if his dinner wasn't ready or if there wasn't enough food for him on his plate.

At weekends, he'd drive my (support worker) car if we went out (I still couldn't drive). When I talked to him about getting a job, he wouldn't allow it.

Looking back, he was just so controlling. There was one time I wanted to get keyboard lessons but he wouldn't let me and shouted at me when I tried to book them on the phone.

In the end, I got a keyboard with lights to follow as a learning aid. It wasn't what I wanted.

Every aspect of my life was being controlled. Being with him was worse than being with the support workers.

Chapter 21

Learning to drive (2009)

By Katie

Despite our relationship difficulties, my boyfriend and I discussed having children, but agreed that I needed to learn to drive first.

At the beginning of 2009 I started my driving lessons, using lots of different instructors! I found the gears too difficult so eventually moved on to an automatic car which made it a lot easier.

It took me seven attempts to pass my theory test but I kept at it and soon it was time for my actual driving test.

On the 14 December 2009 I had my first test. I was really nervous but I passed!

I wanted to get a car as soon as possible so I could tell my Mum and Dad on Christmas Day. I spoke to my solicitor, Yasmin, as I needed some more money transferring over to pay for the car.

I was very excited to surprise my family on Christmas Day. It was very icy and I shared the driving to my Mum and Dad's bungalow with my boyfriend.

We knocked on the door and, when they answered, I shouted "I passed first time!" and showed them my driving licence.

My Dad was really pleased and went straight out to look at the car, but my Mum didn't smile or say anything. I don't know why.

Chapter 22

Getting engaged and having a baby (2010/11)

By Katie

After I'd passed my driving test we started to try for a baby.

First, I had to see my doctor, who confirmed it was okay for me to have a child but said I would need four scans instead of two so they could keep a close eye on the baby's progress.

In May 2010, I discovered I was pregnant!

We were really excited to tell our parents. We went to see my parents first as they lived nearer. We decided to wait until they asked if we'd like a cup of tea and then say "yes please, Grandma and Grandad". I remember my Dad being over the moon, although Mum didn't say much. My boyfriend's parents were surprised and pleased as well.

The next three months were a total nightmare though. I was so tired but my boyfriend was no help at all.

In the time I was pregnant I started seeing shadows and I know very well it was an angel or someone from my family. Not all people believe that sort of thing but I do. I started doing the garden once and suddenly I felt someone pointing on my shoulder. I turned around and no one was there and I know my boyfriend was upstairs painting so it must have been someone. They were all there to support me and keep me going.

Although we went away and stayed in a lodge for my birthday in June, my boyfriend spent most of the time fishing. When he wasn't fishing, he was shouting at me.

I remember my boyfriend coming in one day after he'd been fishing and shouting at me because there wasn't any food in the house. He stormed out to the fish and chip shop and locked me inside the lodge. I was really frightened - I don't know what I would have done if there had been a fire.

On the day of my birthday, we went out for a meal. When I picked up the bill (I always paid!) I saw a box there and knew it was an engagement ring. My boyfriend went down on one knee and asked me to marry him. I said yes but what a mistake it turned out to be.

Our baby was due in the middle of December 2010. One Saturday night in December we were watching the X Factor final with a takeaway. I'd ordered curry and had a raw pineapple and was drinking plenty of water.

As I walked up the stairs, my waters broke. We grabbed my bag and went straight to the hospital.

When we got to hospital, we were taken to a room where we waited. Eventually, I was taken upstairs to the ward on a bed. This is when the pain really started. I got a terrible kicking pain in my back and, when this stopped, I got the same kicking pain in my front. I also couldn't stop going to the toilet as my waters broke.

The next day, I can remember sitting up on the bed with the doctor and student nurse, and lots of other nurses there. My boyfriend was also there. The student nurse put a needle in my back. I heard him say the words "Is that where it goes?" and then I was unconscious.

When I opened my eyes, I had a mask on my mouth and there were lots of people around me. There was something in front of me so I couldn't see past my stomach. I couldn't see my boyfriend anywhere either.

I kept taking the mask off and asking if my baby was okay. The nurses then moved me into another room and brought in my baby. My boyfriend was sitting next to me and we welcomed our baby boy into the world. It was a magical moment. We called him Liam.

Sadly, nothing changed with my boyfriend after Liam was born. He was still moody and angry with me most of the time. He didn't help with Liam either. I might as well have been on my own.

One time I had terrible tonsillitis and a sore throat. I was on medication. Liam needed to be changed and fed so I ask if my boyfriend if he could do it as I was not very well. He just snapped back "I'm tired as well I've been to work". It was the same story time and time again. Whenever Liam needed anything, it was all down to me.

Liam's christening was on 11 February 2011. On the day of the christening my friend Julie had arrived to do my hair for me. My Dad then arrived and said Mum felt dizzy and had been put on medication the same as me as they said it was an epileptic fit. So, because of that, Mum and Dad didn't come to the christening.

After the christening, we all went back to my house and my boyfriend and I announced our wedding date. Outside I was smiling, but inside I was crying, thinking "what am I doing?".

Bev left after the christening as well. My boyfriend never liked Bev and kept telling me again and again to tell her to go. It wasn't the nicest thing to do.

Chapter 23

Wedding bells and tears of sadness (2012)

By Katie

Getting ready for our wedding was stressful and it was made even worse by my boyfriend's behaviour towards me.

I'd always wanted to get married (to the right person) and dreamt of arriving at the church in a horse drawn carriage, having a reception in a posh hotel and going on honeymoon somewhere hot.

In the run up to the wedding, my boyfriend continued to shout at me over all sorts of things, including the seating plan and my hen night. We were constantly arguing and I often thought about cancelling the whole thing. My family had also picked up on how he was controlling me.

I paid for the church and my Mum and Dad paid for the reception, which was really expensive. My boyfriend also persuaded me to open a joint wedding account which meant he could access my money. He didn't contibute anything!

The evening before the wedding I was in my bedroom at Mum and Dad's place with a cuppa. My head was just spinning around and I wanted to cry, but I had to act as normal.

On the morning of the wedding, I was terrified of what I was letting myself in for. After I'd had my hair done, we all went back to my Mum and Dad's. Soon it was time to put on my wedding dress which was gorgeous. I'd picked a burgundy colour dress for my bridesmaid Claire (sister) and the flowers were the same colour.

I was excited when I saw the horse carriage arrive but on the way to the church, I just gritted my teeth and tried not to cry. Dad was having a whale of time waving at everyone like a King, bless him!!

We got to the church I got out of the carriage and made my way inside with Dad and Claire behind me. I was so nervous walking down the aisle.

When we got to the point where it was time to say "I do", I started crying. Everyone thought they were happy tears, but the opposite was true. But it was too late to go back. Rather than signing the paper with my name I wish I'd written "get lost".

Even at the reception afterwards I felt physically sick. My boyfriend - now my husband - made a speech, but it was all a pack of lies.

On my wedding night - supposedly the happiest day of my life - I went to bed staring at the ceiling and asking myself "what have I done".

When it came to our honeymoon, I had no say at all.

We stayed in an old-fashioned house with a lake so, of course, my husband could go fishing - which he did most of the time.

Liam was with us although he got really ill one day and we had to call the emergency doctor. Thankfully, he recovered and was fine.

Almost straight after our honeymoon, my husband wanted to get a bigger house. I didn't see why we needed a bigger house but, as usual, he was insistent.

One day I went to look at a house, which had stables, with my Mum. When I got home, he went absolutely ballistic. I went to my bedroom and cried and cried.

Instead, my husband found a big 5-bedroom house with lots of land. It even had space for a swimming pool and tennis court. He wanted his name on the paperwork even though I was paying for the property. I knew very well that Yasmin, my solicitor, wouldn't let that happen, but he kept going on it was going through. At this point I was confused. It never happened though - Yasmin would not let it go through.

Chapter 24

Abuse and separation (2013/2014)

By Katie

In September 2013 we went on a caravan holiday with Liam.

Again, and as usual, I paid for everything.

One evening we got a takeaway. I must have done something wrong as my husband started shouting at me. I was crying while he just laughed back at me.

During the night, it was always me who went to Liam when he cried or needed settling.

The whole time, I had to do whatever my husband wanted. For legal reasons - and to protect Liam - I won't go in to the appalling details. But the abuse was physical as well as emotional. And it went on and on and on.

It was too much to take and I decided to leave him.

I went to see My mum and told her everything and that I wanted him to go. On the day, I asked my Sister and her boyfriend to be there or he wouldn't have gone.

When I got home, Liam had gone round to my Mum and Dad's – he was too young to know what was going on in any case. That wasn't an easy day.

We sorted custody arrangements through the solicitor and agreed that Liam would go to his Dad's house every other weekend and to his Nan and Grandad's house every Wednesday for dinner. Later on, my ex wanted to have Liam every other Friday as well. I didn't particularly like it but it had to happen.

Following our separation, Christmas 2013 was particularly hard. I had Liam on Christmas Day and we went to his Dad's house on Boxing Day - an arrangement we kept moving forward.

My husband also owed me £3,000 he used for a new car from the joint account we had set up for the wedding - more really as he only gave me £30 a week and nothing for food, bills or Liam.

While he told his Mum and Dad he was paying me back I didn't believe him so I went to the bank with Mum to find out. There was a long queue in the bank and I was very nervous. When the cashier told me that the money hadn't been paid back, I burst into tears and fell to the floor. I just couldn't control my emotions anymore.

Thankfully, our divorce was finalised in 2014. Dealing with the solicitors and sorting everything out was really stressful and I'd often burst into floods of tears. It was a really horrible experience.

Chapter 25

My own business (2015)

By Katie

When I was pregnant, I'd started buying beads and tools from a craft shop to make jewellery.

I enjoyed making necklaces, bracelets and earrings in all the colours that match.

I made one for my Mum's birthday and when she wore it to work, one of her colleagues asked if I could make one for her too. Soon, more and more people were showing an interest.

So, after my divorce, I decided to book a table at a local craft fair. We called our table Beautiful Beads and made some pink business cards.

On the day of the fair I was very nervous and happy at the same time.

The fair was packed and I sold lots as well as collecting quite a few orders to do at home. It was a three-day fair so Dad came over and helped us. By the end of the fair, we were all exhausted!

Following the first fair, Mum and I went to lots of other fares in all sorts of places. My little business was really taking off!

As my jewellery sales continued, I turned my garage into a work room and then, in November 2015, I found my own shop

While I was doing craft fairs, I started looking for a puppy instead of a dog. I found a 6-month-old black Labrador who was already trained. When I did the fairs at the weekend my sister came over to check on my puppy.

I didn't want to leave the puppy with Liam on his own (he was in pre-school at the time) so sometimes we had to keep him in a cage which wasn't fair. One night when Liam was in bed, I let the puppy out and it went absolutely ballistic, running round and growling. I was absolutely terrified and had to send him back to the old owners. It was upsetting.

Chapter 26

My own shop (2016/2017)

By Katie

It was really exciting to have my own shop.

The room we were renting was at a Garden Centre, in a huge glass building.

In the winter we needed to wear plenty of clothes, take lots of blankets, and use a gas heater. In the summer, we were roasting and had to get lots of air conditioning units!

As I'd starting making jewellery in crystals, I changed the name of the business to Beautiful Jewellery Designs.

After we had decorated and got some furniture to put my jewellery on we advertised our opening day and lots of people come along, including my Aunt and Uncle. I was totally exhausted by the end of the day!

As the shop got busier, we hired an assistant to help with the paperwork.

Soon I started to sell healing stones and crystals and took a Diploma in Crystal Healing which helped me to explain everything to our customers.

For an example, on one occasion two ladies came in to my shop. They had a look around and saw my healing stones. I went over to talk to them about healing stones and what they can do. Not all people believe they will help you but after I did my crystal cards for them and the looked at my Crystal Bible Book, they changed their mind and bought the healing stones. They also came back after a few weeks and the lady said that she got very attracted to a particular food that she didn't normally eat.

I also started repairing jewellery as there wasn't a place nearby.

Mum then came up with the idea of doing workshops at the shop, teaching people how to make all sorts of different jewellery.

I'd been teaching my Mum to make jewellery as well and she had another idea to go on The Craft Shop which is on YouTube. I was very nervous!

When I was at the garden centre and Liam had just started school, I got another puppy. He didn't work out either as he was running around in the morning when I was trying to get Liam ready for school and leaving a little brown present on the floor! That was a no no so he went back to the owners.

While the shop was really great, it was a 45-minute journey from home 6 days a week (I had Monday off). So we started to look for somewhere closed to home. Thankfully we found a place right in the village and close to Liam's school.

Chapter 27

Moving on (2018/2019)

By Katie

20th July 2018 was our last Friday at the old shop so we had the removal van booked. My new shop, Beautiful Jewellery Designs, was in the old Primary School - although it was now called the Community Hub and Library (my old cleaning job).

Our first day was busy and we sold a lot. As time went on Mum had the idea to rent some space in the shop to someone who sold art and crafts.

I was carrying on doing my diploma (in the end I passed with a double A!) and I also did Reiki (a Japanese technique for stress reduction and relaxation that also promotes healing) Level 1 and 2 to become a Reiki practitioner. I then did an Indian Head Massage Practitioner Diploma and passed that as well. We made space in the shop for a special chair / bed for people to have their treatment.

Around this time, I also started singing lessons as I'd just written my own song called 'Moved On'.

My health problems were continuing though. In 2018, I was diagnosed with 'Depression and Anxiety Disorder' and put on medication. My knees were also hurting all the time.

At the end of the year, I went to the doctors about my knee pain. I went privately for a scan .and when the results came back, they told me I had Fibromylia which is caused from stress. The NHS came back with the same results.

The shop was also getting too much for me.

At the end of 2019, I decided to close the shop, everything was getting too much. I know Mum would disagree, so I packed all my things while Mum was on holiday. I ended up having a massive fall out with Mum, just before Christmas. I said some horrible things I'll never forget and always will regret it.

Chapter 28

Losing my mum (2020)

Like everyone, I found the Covid lockdowns really hard – Liam quickly got bored of watching Joe Wicks on YouTube!!

Trying to help Liam with his school work at home was so difficult and everything started to get on top of me.

I found myself exhausted and on the verge of a nervous breakdown again, constantly getting up in the middle of the night with all sorts of suicidal thoughts. It was only Liam who kept me going.

During the lockdown I got in touch with my Mum and we made up - but I was shocked to find out she'd developed throat cancer.

In December 2021, Mum was rushed to hospital and put on oxygen.

At hospital, Mum just wasn't getting any better. One day, Dad phoned me to say that her legs had gone and she was asleep all the time not saying anything.

Then, on another day, Dad called me and was really upset. He'd gone to see Mum and the hospital had said she was not going to get any better and wouldn't survive without the oxygen. Mum went downhill really quickly and was moved to another ward. On the 2nd January 2022. Mum's pain ended when they turned her machine off. She's in heaven now, at peace.

Later in the year, in May, I also lost my 19-year-old cat, Jasmin. It brought all the anguish flooding back.

Afterword

By Katie

Thank you for reading my book.

Since my accident back in 1996, I've been to hell and back.

But, despite everything life has thrown at me, I'm a survivor. For the first time in a long time, I'm also feeling positive about my future.

I also know that in some ways I'm lucky.

If my doctor and air ambulance weren't there when I needed them, I wouldn't be here now to tell you my story. In the aftermath of my brain injury, I had a one in three chance of survival.

I've got a beautiful son, Liam who's now at secondary school. It makes me proud every day to see him growing up.

At the end of last year, I did two Diplomas, one was Chakras and Aura (I got a B) while the other was Connecting with the Spirit Guides (I also got a B). I love to help and heal, whether through Reiki or Healing Stones. I know a lot more now about connecting with spirits and I know my Mum is proud of what I have done.

My health will always be a battle. I'm managing my fibromyalgia as best I can and I've also overcome my anxiety and depression.

I wanted to write this book to show you how dangerous head injury can be. On the news, it shows how people with brain injury can recover in a few months or maybe a year, but I had to start my whole life again and it has taken me so many years to get where I am now. You really wouldn't want to go through what I have.

After I finished writing this book, I started doing abstract art and I've started my own YouTube channel where I can show you what I've done and how I've done it. I'll also show you how to make jewellery as I have many pearls, wire etc left. It will be called Katie's True Story.

Writing this book has helped me a lot. By reading it, you've also helped me more than you'll ever know.

Love, Katie.

Acknowledgements

I would like to say a huge thank you to a lot of people.

First is Kieron Wiscombe who was my doctor and was volunteering as a first responder for L.I.V.E.S. that day.

Thank you to all the paramedics who were working in the air ambulance that day.

Thank you to Jonathan and his assistant, Maria who performed the operation at the Queen's Medical Centre in Nottingham, and to all the doctors and nurses.

When I moved to Pilgrim Hospital in Boston thank you to everyone there - Sister Margaret, Vick the play leader, the physiotherapists, school teachers, nurses and doctors, occupational therapists, speech therapists, and Dr Crawford.

Thank you to my teachers, all the staff, and the speech therapist at Moor House Boarding School in Surrey.

Thank you to all the support workers, case managers and especially Yasmin Ameer my solicitor, who has been there from the start. When I've been on my own she has always been there when I needed anything.

Then my last big thank you is to my Mum and Dad who were with me 24 hours in the hospitals.

Thank you to the rest of family who have supported Mum and Dad.

Even though mum has passed away she is watching and knows what I am doing.

Printed in Great Britain
by Amazon

28768434R00066